FRIENDZ

Written & Un-Edited
by Darick Spears

FRIENDZ

ISBN: 978-1-954133-01-3

GET YOUR BOOK WRITTEN & PUBLISHED TODAY BY

DARICK SPEARS

EMAIL: DARICK@DDSMEDIAWORKS.COM

CALL 414-988-4946

I HAVE BEEN USED AND
ABUSED,
LONELY, MISCONSTRUED,
AND NOW I SIT
CONTEMPLATIVE IN MY CHAIR
CONFUSED.
PONDERING,
WHAT IS A TRUE FRIEND?

The money breeds envy,
The smile brings jealousy.
The honesty can cause
animosity.
So, I stay to myself,
But still in search of a true
friend.

WE ALL GET BIT BY THE LOVE
BUG,
STUNG BY THE SELF-CONSCIOUS
BEE.
BUT WE ALL YEARN TO HAVE
COMPANIONSHIP,
SOMEONE WE CAN CALL A TRUE
FRIEND INDEED.

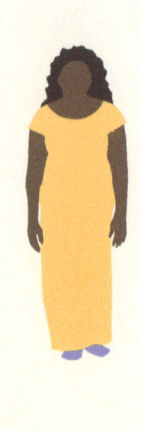

IF THEY TELL YOU LIES,
THEN THEY ARE NOT YOUR
FRIEND.
IF THEY TALK ABOUT YOU
BEHIND YOUR BACK,
THEN YOU SHOULD NOT CALL
THEM FRIEND.

To **make a** friend,
You must show
yourself to be friendly.
With no judgment,
Provide **a handshake**
with a cup
that is empty.
And **stick around** when
the times get windy.

Happy Hour.

Here and now,
Be present.
Be wise not in your own eyes,
Be legend.
Your friends and your
enemies,
Stay **10 steps** ahead of them.

Grab a bite to eat.
Embrace a laugh and a hug.
Abandon your negative inner thoughts.
Call up a friend and have a conversation.

As sweet **as a good watermelon**

As passionate as an activist,

So is that **of a good friend**.

An answer of honesty,

A secret ear that will listen,

A closed mouth after a **deep**

revelation.

So is that of a good friend.

Have you ever lost one?
Have you ever gained one?
Two different emotions.
Two different valuable journeys.
One filled with memories,
The other embodies the process of
making them.
Both important.
Both Priceless.

The highs.
The lows.
The balance of life.

BUT ON YOUR JOURNEY,
BE SURE TO MAKE
PLENTY OF FRIENDZ.

Never take a good one <u>for granted.</u>
Never waste your energy on those phony ones.
True friendship is sacred.
What a friend we have in Jesus.

TODAY

True love is a **paradox,** Because love ignores the truth, **For we** all are imperfect, **Selfish,** And from our loved ones we hide what is true.

YOU CAN **SEARCH HIGH** AND LOW,
YOU CAN EVEN CHECK BETWEEN **THE EARTH'S** MOST SACRED CREVICES,
AND YET YOU WILL NOT FIND ANYTHING **MORE DEAR** THAN A TRUE FRIEND.

IMPORTANT!

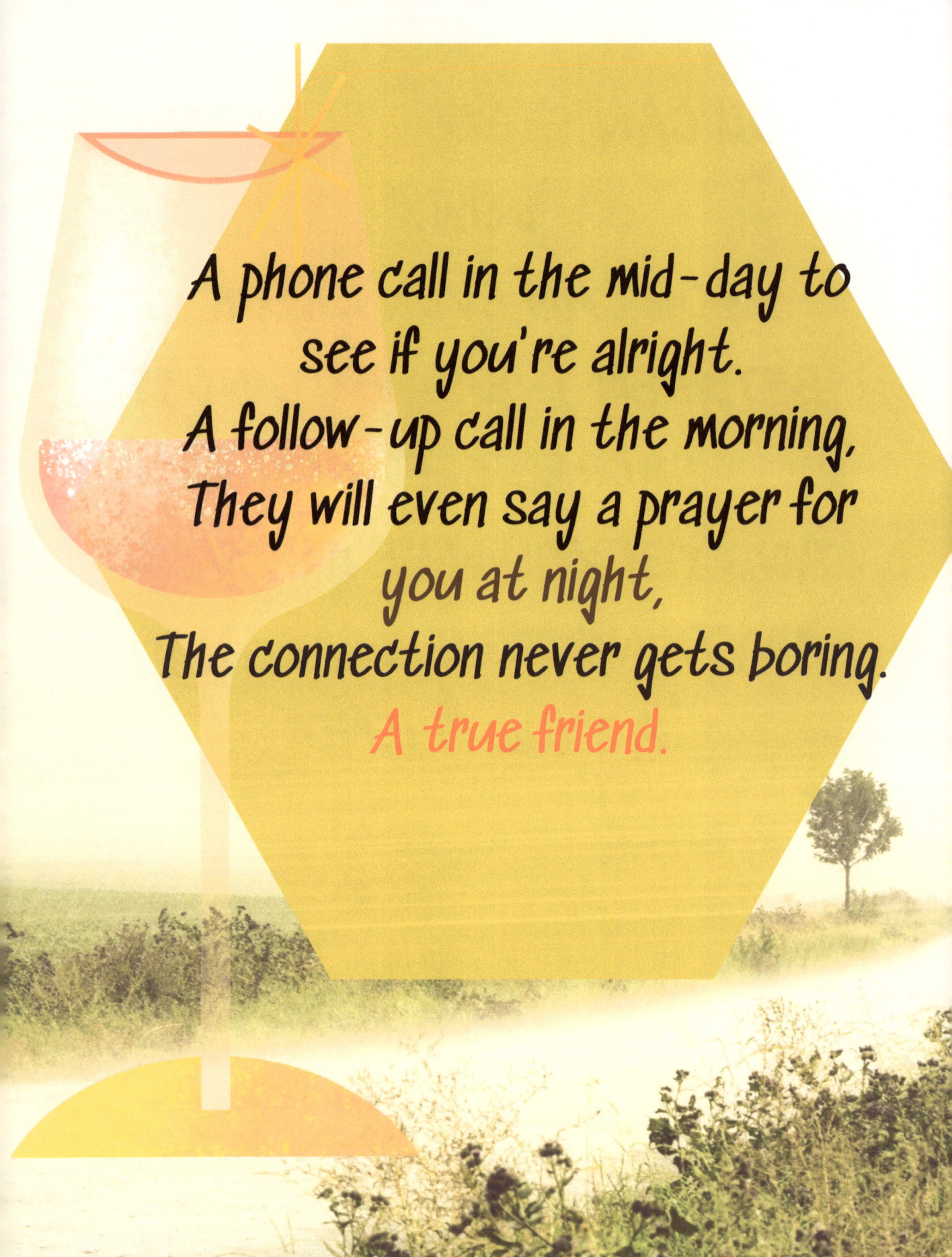

A phone call in the mid-day to see if you're alright.
A follow-up call in the morning,
They will even say a prayer for you at night,
The connection never gets boring.
A true friend.

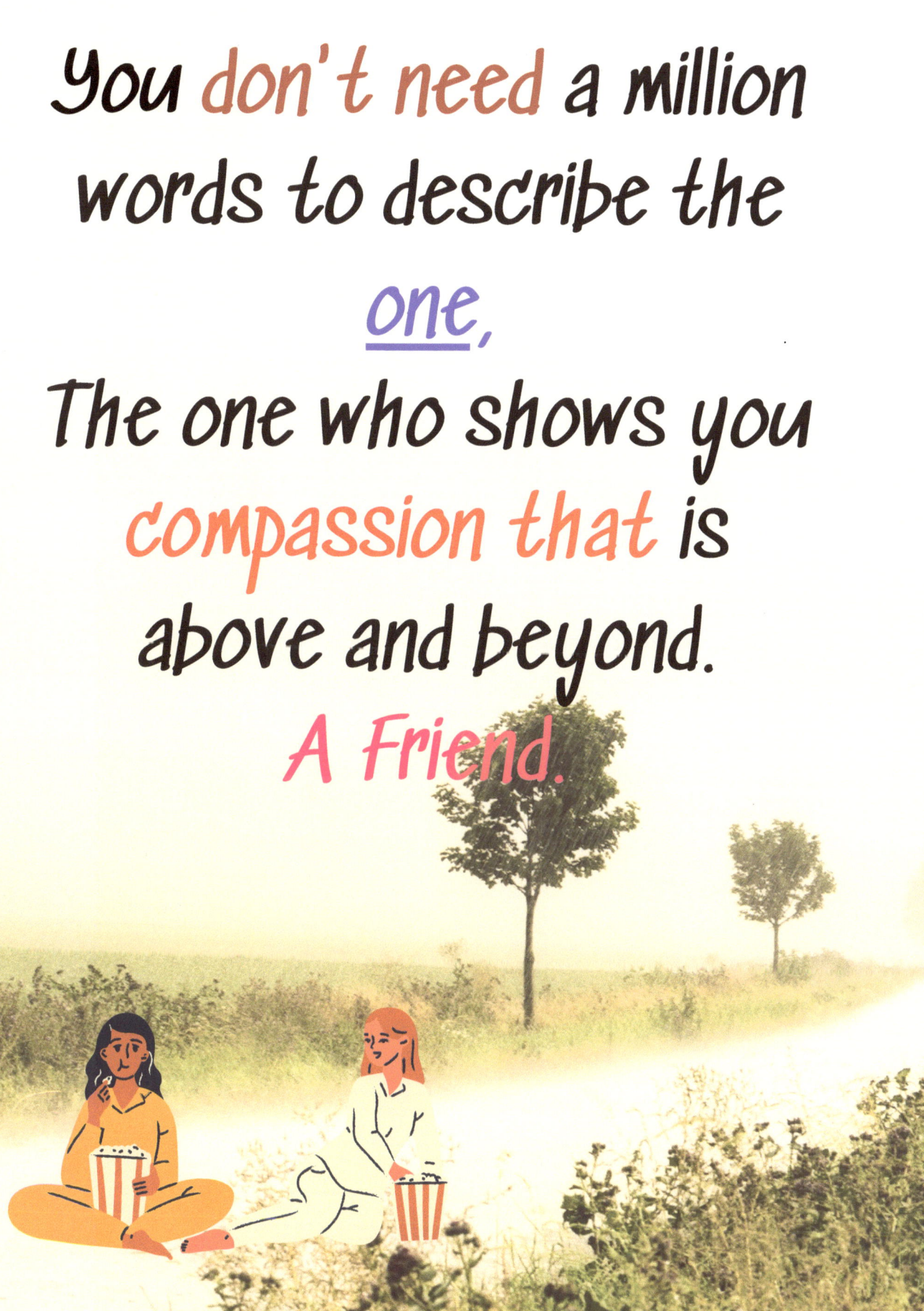

You *don't need* a million words to describe the
<u>one</u>,
The one who shows you
compassion that is
above and beyond.
A Friend.

The **combination of trust** and sincerity,
In this day in time that is a rarity.
Honor.
Loyalty.
The ingredients to a great friend.

I LOST AND GAINED SOME,
WAS HURT, SCARRED, AND
PARALYZED.
TIME HEALED THOSE WOUNDS.
BUT MY MEMORIES STILL
HUNT ME.
STILL SOME UNANSWERED
QUESTIONS.
WERE THEY REALLY
FRIENDZ?

IN A DESERT WITH THOUGHTS,
FORCED TO FACE MY OWN
FEARS.
WISHING I COULD PICK UP
THE PHONE AND HEAR YOUR
VOICE AGAIN.
BUT ALL I CAN HEAR IS YOUR
WHISPERS IN THE WIND.

WE ALL NEED ONE ANOTHER,
ONE HAND WASHES THE OTHERS
FOOT.

HUMILITY.

SERVICE.

A GOOD NEIGHBOR.

A FRIEND.

LET'S TAKE A WALK.
LET'S HAVE A NICE TALK.
LET'S CHERISH THE MOMENTS.
LET'S NOT FORGET THAT WE
ARE LIVING ON BORROWED
TIME.
LET ME GIVE YOU THOSE
FLOWERS WHILE YOU ARE
STILL HERE.

HEY!
THANKS FOR BEING A FRIEND.

Darick Books